luminous

POEMS & INQUIRY FOR THE SOUL'S JOURNEY
LAURA WEAVER

Luminous

First published in 2018
by SoulPassages Press
Boulder, CO 80302 USA

Copyright ©2018 by Laura Weaver

All rights reserved. This book, or parts thereof, may not be reproduced in any form without permission. For information contact Laura at WeaverPoetry@gmail.com

Book Design/Interior Layout: Suzanne Nason, Twistology.com
Author Photo: Simon Alexander
Cover Photo: Getty Images

ISBN # 978-0-692-14669-9

LUMINOUS
POEMS & INQUIRY FOR THE SOUL'S JOURNEY

LAURA WEAVER

SoulPassages Press
Boulder, Colorado
2018

Dedication

I dedicate this book to my mentors, teachers and guides who have taught me about the Path of the Heart, the Language of the Soul, and the Alchemy of Light and Dark.

I dedicate this book to my children Simon and Mariah— and to the next generations who will inherit this precious earth at this transformational time in our evolution.

I offer this book as my soul song and deepest prayer.

TO **YOU**

I invite you to enter this house of poetry: **Luminous**. Please bring your own heart, soul, body and wisdom to this journey. Each poem is meant as an invitation to deeper awareness and awakening.

These poems are seeds, prayers, droplets from the river of life, sparks from Mystery's ever burning fire. May each of us know our soul gifts, purpose, belonging, and awakened heart.

These poems are written to be shared, to be read aloud, to be read multiple times. They are multi-faceted and reveal themselves more deeply upon repeating—in part, because of the alchemy that happens when you bring your stories, visions, dreams, and associations to them. I see you—readers—as soul friends on the path, kin in a heart-full conversation, companion dancers in the great Dance.

The flow of the poems through the four sections of the book provides a roadmap for the journey of the soul. Section I, **Initiation**, includes poems about the initiatory passages of life—those moments of transformation, shift, and rupture where Life asks us to let go of the familiar and leap into the unknown—so that we may discover new ways of being and understanding. Section II, **Revelation**, explores the gifts and power of wild places (within and without) and the ways we are seasoned by the seasons of our lives. Section III, **Creation**, offers poems that speak to our own personal mythos and origin stories—to the elements that have shaped who we are and what we are here to do and be. The final section, **Awakening**, includes poems that celebrate the Dance with the Divine—and the experience of what it is to be both mortal and infinite. It is my hope that in each of these sections you will find chords or echoes from your own stories, lives and experiences.

After each poem, you will find a few reflection questions to support you to make your own personal connections to the poems. Please—journal, inquire, ask questions, wonder, dream alongside these poems. Write your own soul poems. It is up to **all** of us to keep the language of the soul alive in this era of sound bites, commodification, and soul numbing over-stimulation and trauma.

In the beginning, there was the Word. In the beginning there was the Song. And at this time of both profound endings and miraculous new beginnings, may we re-member the Soul of the World together—and sing ourselves home.

CONTENTS

ONE: **INITIATION**

12	The Inner Temple
13	The Story
14	Unmasked
16	Making Passage
17	The Vow
18	Sacred Wound
19	Turning Towards
20	Soul Wringing
21	True Names
22	Fire & Water
23	First Flight
24	Source

TWO: **REVELATION**

26	Revelation
27	Beauty
28	One Drop
29	Beyond the Breakwaters
30	Pilgrimage to Blue Lake
31	Murmuration
32	Chinook
33	Winter's Dreaming
34	Solstice
35	Clematis
36	Rewilding
37	A Way of Walking

THREE: **CREATION**

40 House of Origin
42 Arrival
43 Current
44 Eleven
45 The Library of the Body
46 Net of Dreams
47 Visitation
48 Lineage
50 Creation Stories
52 Remembering our Descendants
54 The Feast
56 Forgiveness

FOUR: **AWAKENING**

58 The Boat
60 Surrender
61 Heart Sutra
62 Alchemy
63 Love Poem from God
64 Where the Honey is Stored
65 Without Exile
66 Eye of the Moon
68 Luminous
70 The Empty Bowl
72 The Ocean Inside
73 Cornucopia

initiation

The Inner Temple

We are only asked
to follow the spiral down and in,
to leave the outer world behind
just for a breath, just for a minute—
to touch our lips to the sweet springs
that bubble up from this refuge.

This, not simply a delight,
but a requirement—if we wish
to walk in the world in our wholeness—
not as hungry ghosts forever
seeking the elusive watering hole—
but as a *presence* inhabited by *presence*.

Here, the temple walls, illuminated,
show us the maps home.
Here, the hidden scriptures reveal themselves
in our cells as Original Instructions.
Here, the light recognizes itself
and heals the first wound of separation.

In this chamber within, we are washed
clear of our burdens by starlight, returned
to the sanctuary of our own essence,
broken open like the milkweed pod—
our seeds streaming forth on the wind.

reflections
~What does your inner temple look and feel like? How do you access it?
~What Original Instructions are written in your inner temple—and how can they guide your life?

The Story

Step closer to the story that scares you—
the one that has you gasping for air
in the night, searching for ground.
This one wants to take you past
the lip of the void to the birthplace
of stars, where all stories dissolve
into the blessing of original song.

Turn your wild horses out
into the fields in the morning,
when first light purples the hills.
They are hungry for this earth
under hoof, this thunder of full gallop.
They may trample all the places
you have so carefully tended.
They may leave you in a cloud of dust.
And yet, this is the only way
they will return to you truly,
without a fence to keep them in.

Leap into the love that terrifies—
you know just what it will do.
It will un-hinge every door in your house.
It will blow in like a hurricane
and re-arrange your furniture.
It will howl through your bones
and leave you delightfully hollow.
Without this love you are only playing
at this life– and you are so tired of that!

Let the current lift you
out of the churning eddy.
There is only one place where this river flows—
through slot canyons and the eyes of midnight,
through singing valleys and greening glens.
These blessed waters will have their way with you.
They are dreaming you into a body of light.
Why fight what you most long for?

reflections
~What is the "story that scares you" in your life? How might you step closer to this story?
~How does Love wish to rearrange your life?

Unmasked

It is our inheritance to learn
the many ways to stitch the self together
with knots and ties and fishing hooks
to create an identity with all
we have on hand—
tissue paper and glue
hardwood and chisel
bravado and vehemence—
until we have made a beautiful mask,
a likeness so intricate
we trick ourselves
into a kind of deep forgetting.

We wear that mask
as if it is our original face—
the one that came before the stars.
But just as the acorn knows
the oak it will become,
and the apple seed encodes
the evolutionary pulse of the next tree
within the fruit of its last season,
something within us *remembers*.

It is only a matter of time
before life taps a tiny hammer
along the seams, before we can dig
our fingers around the edges
to pry the false self loose.
It is only a matter of time
before we find the second mask
under the first. And then the third
under the second. And then, yes—
like the onion peeled to luminous emptiness,
we find the unfamiliar shape of our face
before we were born.

We did not imagine we could be this free.
And here, revealed, we understand
what the moon and sun know—
that we are reflections of reflections.
That we can choose to live forever
in a maze of mirrors, or find
what howls at the center
of our own inner labyrinth.

Here, we meet the unmasked one—
the one who has never
been harmed, betrayed, or broken.
Here, we meet the one
who carries our medicine
and knows the many names for Holy.

reflections
~What are the various masks you have worn in this life? Which masks are you currently wearing?
~Who is the "unmasked one"—and what gifts or medicine does this one of you carry?

Making Passage

It's like swimming across a river
with our eyes closed, this passage
through the center of our life.

Sometimes we have to navigate
from the inside out—when the stars
hide their light, when we cannot see

the bank on the other side, when the hounds
of our past bark on the shoreline,
braying their mournful song at our leaving.

It is the stillness at the center of the fire
that guides—the voice of our angel of mercy
that rings out when we look over our shoulder

at the old life with longing. *You cannot go back*,
she says, *that place is gone now*. And for a moment,
we freeze in the river sure we will drown,

forgetting which way is up and down,
forward and back, as the roar of the roiling rapids
pours through us, the heart filled

with all the questions that have refused
to leave us alone. And then something
remembers itself, lifts our shoulders above

the swirling cauldron of in-between,
and we simply let go of the fight to stay.
The tangled paradoxes flow on through

the body of the river, and we are carried
by an invisible current that draws us closer
and closer to the edge of a new world.

On our knees, we find root and ground,
give thanks for this fertile soil, seeded
with our dreams, thirsty for our arrival.

reflections
~What passage are you in the midst of right now?
~What questions "refuse to leave you alone?"

The Vow

It was the chasm below the towering cliffs
that called me that spring morning to climb—
step by step—into a knowing of what I must do.

Burning in my ears was the fierce song of a vow
I had made long ago—not to bend the truth inside
or live forever in a house of mirrors.

There, perched on the granite rocks,
I listened to the high, insistent cheeping of peregrines
sounding out like this forgotten one of me.

And as I watched, out of the stone spires, the mother falcon
shot fast and hard, dove down deep into the soul
of that canyon—the ribbon of riverlight moving far below.

She showed me a thing or two about the source
of my own desire—the glint of her arrowed wings, the heat
of her body searing the air. And just before certain death,

she caught a swallow in her beak, rose to circle
these impossible heights, then slid into an invisible crack
in the cliff to feed her newborns—still crying out

as if they had been forgotten. What it is to be half-blind,
vulnerable, hungry for the world, not yet seeing
the coming fledge, but knowing—deep in the bones—

the compass of primal instinct. What it is to know just how
to ride the current at full speed, to lift before colliding,
to break buoyant into that late afternoon light—

wings thrumming, filled with the ecstasy
of your own mysterious wild.

reflections
~What essential vows have you made to yourself?
~How are you fulfilling these vows...or not?

Sacred Wound

In every being there lives a wound.
This is the nature of being born here,
in a body, like this.

And in every life there is a choice—
to wrap ourselves around that wound,
protective of its shape, its cadence, its nuance—
to build our life around that story,
or to extend through the fire of pain
to a new horizon.

The seed knows this: how to arise
from the dark tight curl
of the pod to break ground.
As does the monarch,
as it emerges from the chaos
of its own dissolution
into winged delight.

It is the impossible miracle
of the heart that brings us
to the hearth of our own awakening—
that risks broaching illusory walls,
that opens against all odds—
seeing we have nothing to lose
but our own false protection,
our own holding back.

In every being there is a wound—
a fissure where sacred longing is born—
so our gifts can be revealed,
so our gifts can be given.

reflections
~What is the central or core wound in your story and in your life?
~What sacred longing or gift has been born from this wound—and how does it wish to be given or expressed?

Turning Towards

No matter how many times we shed,
no matter how far and wide the spirit has soared,
no matter how deeply the body knows
the galloping hooves of our own wild horse—

there are days when we look in the mirror and see
grief, shell shock, the fingers of time working our face
like clay. There are days we forget our own name.
The tears come as medicine, truth, nectar.

Impermanence topples all of our dreams—
even the beautiful ones. When the bottom
falls out, when the foundation shifts,
when the seismic quake rolls through—

we know we are no-*thing* that can be counted,
that death lives with us in every breath,
that the self is a blessed vessel cracked with starlight.
And how is it that just as we release our grip,

just as we surrender to this *emptiness*,
just as we turn to what is most unbearable—
a sea bird flies in and begins to build a nest,
one stick at a time, in the center of the heart?

Soon there are brilliant blue eggs!
How is this so?

reflections
~What grief and shell shock live in your body?
~When you turn towards your own grief or heartache—what "brilliant blue eggs" do you find there?

Soul Wringing

In the dream, a wise man and I fall to the earth
laughing over nothing—our bellies quaking
on warm soil, the air filled with our wonder.

He has recently been to the edge of death—
his body riddled with parasites,
and now—miraculously well again.

I ask him what his illness taught him.
And he says: *It was a soul wringing—*
my soul wrung out of every pride,

every arrogance, every prized accolade.
I see it in his face—the way this journey
has brought back his joy, how he was restored

by letting go of what seemed most precious—
how he can now give himself all
he could never before receive.

In the dream, this man is a beloved teacher
and I, a kind of daughter learning the ways
to whole my own heart. And this soul wringing—

not some penance or punishment,
but more of a gracious peacemaking—
where each morning I gather dew

from the tongues of grass
and drink each drop—one by one.

reflections
~What crisis or challenging event has given you an opportunity to engage in "soul wringing?"
~What peacemaking do you wish to invite into your heart and life?

True Names

I learned my true name
from the sea—from the swing
of the tides and the glint
of moonlight over the wash
of grunion running at midnight.

I heard this same name sung out
in a recurring dream,
where I turned my body inside out
to spin a spiral shell—
so I could ride the beauty
of the fierce surf without harm.
This is not a metaphor.

In the wilds of the earth,
everything is symbolic
and yet nothing is abstract.
Nothing stands between
essence and expression.
And the call of this world is to live
as primal revelation, embodied—
as pure presence unveiled.

The sea carries stories
of thousands of storms and sunrises—
of eons when there was only
its own tidal heartbeat to listen to.
The sea carries the memory
of that first evolutionary impulse
that sparked life to leap
from old body to new—
to learn to drink oxygen
and grow legs, lungs, fur.

This same lightning lives
in our cells as this unstoppable love,
as this soul image that shapes
our true name
and will not let us forget
that every facet of this world
sees us. Whoever you are—
you cannot hide
from your belonging.

reflections
~What recurring dreams, visions, or experiences have given you insight about your own true name(s)?
~What does it mean to you to truly belong to the world? If, without a doubt, you felt your belonging to this life and world, what would shift for you?

Fire & Water

For so many years, I only knew initiation by fire—the blaze
that bursts the husks of seeds within, the revelation that turns
dormant longing into rapturous flight. These seeds—

tempered by flame—crack granite, thrive on sheer mountainsides,
find impossible crevasses to call home. I still bear the scars
from the places where fire entered, breaking me open to endless sky.

But now there is another initiation that calls. In this path,
there is a welling up of light from the dark depths, the return
of ancient rivers after long periods of heat and drought.

In this way, gentle waters seep through the hard places, soften
and dissolve the pod—so that the life inside simply emerges.
These seeds require a long drenching rain, the coaxing of sunlight—

a gentle unveiling—until delicate petals unfold one by one—
and the whole hungry world slows down to take a single breath.
And these two kinds of initiations—the fire and the water—

are like two arrows in the bow of the divine archer—who knows
just where the bullseye is—and how to touch the center
of our center where our most intimate secrets dwell.

reflections
~In your life, what kinds of soul initiations have you experienced? What has been revealed?
~What intimate secrets dwell in the center of the center of your being?

First Flight

The clear bead at the center changes everything. There are no edges to my loving now.
Rumi, "Open Secret"

There were edges to my loving—
places where countries clashed along borders,
where lovers were not admitted,
where the thicket grew thick and impenetrable
to keep out savage creatures ambling
about in the dark, smelling of musk.

There were edges to my loving—
places to guard, gardens to endlessly tend—
the project of myself that took such devotion—
voices in my head I did not want heard
by another who might lean over in the night
and kiss away such tender uncertainties.

There were edges to my loving—
there was the wild one of me
who did not want taming,
the one who believed someone
else held the keys to my freedom,
the primal roar of the lioness who said:
*I will belong to no one but myself,
so I cannot belong to you.*

There were edges to my loving.
But then came the tearing wind,
and the sheets of rain, the storms
on the high seas, the sunlight on bare skin,
and the eyes of god blazing through my heart
at dawn. Then came the beasts crashing
through the thickets, despite my best laid plans.
Yes, then came life softening
the edges again and again.

And one night I woke in the night to the sound
of my own laughter, to a knowing of my love
rippling out in endless circles. And in my bones
I felt what has always been free,
this sovereignty that does not require
guarding or liberating. And from here—
belonging to *everything*—I walked out
of the cage of my own making
and tasted true flight for the first time.

reflections
~Where have there been "edges to your loving?" What have you been protecting?
~What has always been free in you? How can you remember that you hold the keys to your own sovereignty and freedom?

Source

La Foux: Cirque de Navelles, France

Deep in the Cévennes mountains
the Vis river flows underground
six miles through a labyrinth
of limestone before re-emerging
so clear and pure, you can lift
your mouth to the opening
and drink straight from the Source.

There are moments of rupture—
we are moving with the river
of our life, when in an instant
we disappear beneath the surface.
We become invisible even
to ourselves, as we are swept *down*
into secret currents that re-imagine
our entire way of being.

How our souls call us again and again
to meet the unknown, to seek our origins,
to look for what cannot be found.
This, the eros of the mystery
that can never be pierced—and we,
the yearning lovers intoxicated
as much by what is hidden
as by what is revealed.

There are some places—
within and without—that are meant
to stay hidden. We catch a glimpse—
we look deep into the shadow
of the stone mouth—to this opening
where the Vis appears anew
after its long descent.

We taste these blessed waters
and are startled into breathing again —
as our own unfamiliar voice
rings out like an oracle, saying:
Drink from the Source—
you too can be re-membered into the light.

reflections

~*When in your life have you been "swept down into secret currents that have re-imagined your entire way of being?"*

~*What in you is ready to be "re-membered into the light?"*

Revelation

Certain wild places appear in your dreams—
sing to you in the middle of the night,

speak your name in between tasks,
so that finally you listen. It is then

you remember how to make a pathway
to meet what calls. Coming with only your faith—

arriving, to find you are noticed.
Fiddleheads unfurl in sunlight.

Mycelial networks quicken
with footfall. Violet butterflies sip

from mud where you press palms
to feel warmth moving in earth again.

This is an ordinary transfiguration.
A simple alchemy. You have whispered

a thousand prayers to get here. You have traveled
a long way in body or soul, to come with hands

outstretched in offering, in longing. When the waves
rush over the rocks, when the tidal pull whips

the silverlight waters into a froth at your feet,
you know that mercy is everywhere.

Your soul is a door, but a doorway to what?
This, the place asks you gently and then relentlessly,

until you empty your pockets of the tangled
fishing lines of lineage and the stories

you thought you must carry—until
you turn yourself inside out to be revealed.

reflections
~What wild places call you—within and without?
~How is your soul a doorway? And where does it lead?

Beauty

There is nowhere to hide in the desert
under the full moon, in the blue light

that pours through the body like water.
It as if we are born again in the open air,

to feel our bare skin against the world
for the first time. And from here, eyes untethered,

we see a different kind of beauty that lives
beneath the surface—that quivers in the thorns

and breaks out of the volcanic rock like a song
you hear when your mind has gone quiet.

To meet this kind of beauty, make a slow approach,
a spiral walk to the center. Leave offerings. Show up

in the odd hours of the night—then she may
let you see her fur, her sharp teeth, the flash

of her pale underbelly. For this kind of beauty moves
in the spaces—in the interior of things, in the rivulets

of a dry land that rarely sees rain, in the seeds
that bloom once in a hundred years, in the sap

of a Joshua tree lifting its arms—heavy with blooms—
to the piercing stars. This beauty leaves you weeping

in the blue of the moonlight
with nowhere to hide.

reflections
~*What beauty lives just beneath the surface or exterior of you?*
~*How do you approach and make relationship with the fierce beauty of the wild—within and without?*

One Drop

In the soft hills of Calistoga,
I walk over ancient lava flows—
the secret to good red wine, I have heard—
this buried ash. Beneath the shadow
of the mountain, vineyards flash
stark crosses—dark
before the resurrection
of summer's first grapes.

Lingering near a stream—just made
by two days and six inches of rain—
she blazes across the path before me.
Oh, to watch the ecstatic thrum
of her humming wings as she hovers
for a long breath, then drops her body
into the rainwater pool,
dipping her jeweled belly
again and again, sipping
on this first nectar of liquid light.

She drinks just long enough,
and then she is gone.
She stays just long enough
to remind me
how little is needed—
how it only takes one drop
to taste the whole of the ocean.

reflections
~Taking the lesson of the hummingbird, where can you sip from the nectar of life?
~What small, quiet moments in your day connect you to the miracle of creation's infinite majesty?

Beyond the Breakwaters

Tulum, Mexico

We ride out on the ebbing tide—oars light through teal waters.
I am singing a melody I have never heard—a song of this threshold place

where calm bay meets open sea, where sheltered life meets infinite wild.
How we come to know ourselves here on the edges, waves surging

over the bow of the boat, the tide drawing us further and further to beyond.
How we go far enough across the shelter of the reef to feel our longing

to surrender to this pull—far enough to know we do not yet belong
to the other side. For hours we dream along the seam of these worlds,

rising and falling with the pulse of tropical rain, the undulation
of iridescent blue fish, the ceremony of green turtle and manta.

For hours we drift just above the jeweled cities of earthbone
and swaying sea-fan—following all that stirs in the depths.

But now, the sun is low—the current stronger, insistent. And our bodies,
like pining lovers, lean towards that forever horizon glimmering

just beyond the breakwaters. But a voice calls us, saying: *It is time
to rudder the boat around. You have been long enough across this veil.*

There is a strange ache when we turn our backs to the open sea.
And a surging forth, too—as the arc of the swells buoy the boat,

carrying us to shore. We are going home to this great invitation
called life—to this mortal world that tears us open again and again,

pouring salt into our wounds until it no longer stings,
pouring salt into our wounds until we are truly healed.

reflections
~What "threshold" or wild places in the natural world evoke a sense of awe in you?
~How is life offering you the very "salt" needed to heal your deepest wounds?

Pilgrimage to Blue Lake

For so many years, you have built elaborate cairns
along the trail to the house of your self.

You have found just the right rocks for balancing,
just the point along the path where you might get lost—

so that in every season, in the deepest snow,
you can find your way back. Each time you come,

you lay a fire on the shoreline with the kindling
of your grief and delight—watch the flames burn slowly

at first—then fast and high as they quicken,
bringing light to dark spaces. And so it is this day,

as you arrive on the shores of Blue Lake, you hear
a different cadence pulsing from the land—

and you wonder if it is time to build a stronger nest
for this next round of seasons, or if it is time to finally fledge.

You stand shaky, barely balanced on the edge
of this and that—while below stretches the great horizon

you long for, though you never believed you could walk
beyond these cairns you have so carefully tended.

And this sacred valley is filled with mist—for the light
has been drinking snow all day long. And in a devastating flash,

you see you must leave this place that has given you all it has.
You have been filled by such beauty, you can no longer stay—

for what is yours to give can no longer be given from here.
And so you take the stones from the cairns,

offer them to the lake and walk off
the edge of all you have ever known.

reflections
~How have you carefully tended the "house of your self?"
~What do you feel called to offer or express in the world that cannot be given from the old version of your self?

Murmuration

In the silver light of dusk, waves
of starlings spark from autumn
bare branches—wingtips painting
hieroglyphics in the blue-black sky.

How each bird tracks the other—
how the many move in one full gesture—
no leading or following, just
this co-emergent dream of flight.

This is the same dance encoded
in our very cells—this is how we know
how to walk through the densest
city streets, how to weave in and out

of bewildering crowds, how to navigate
hallways to find contact and unfold
the flowers of our hands to meet
the most brutal desecrations.

This is our most primary sense
remembered—kinesthetic, relational—
each sovereignty quickened
by the other, each one held

by the many in a glittering web. For we are
not isolated bodies, lost. But a fluid
organism pulsing on currents, inking
the sky with this primal wordless song.

reflections
~Where do you see human beings expressing our capacity for "murmuration"—in which we relate to each other with grace, intelligence and cohesion?

~How can you tap into the experience of being part of a "fluid organism"—and not simply one of many "isolated bodies?"

Chinook

All night I wake again and again
to the jackhammer of my heart,
a tremolo of wind across the plains,
the restlessness of autumn
sliding off the mountains to shake walls,
blast through eaves, tear shingles.

Opening the window, I reach far
beyond the dark, smell the impossible—
honeysuckle fragrant beyond October's freeze.
In a whirl of dry leaves, the willows empty—
their reedy bodies fluting like raging river water.
And beyond the close-in horizon of my life

tree after tree falls in a wake, forests
disappearing as the desert spreads
like a sea. Yes, all across this globe,
villages grow poorer, people thin as branches
from this bark they must eat. This is what
the night shows me, as it lays itself
bonebare—this hunger of wind.

Turning away, I slam the window closed—
search for the sound of childbreath
in nearby rooms. I want the cadence
of May melt, the green leaping forward,
the carnival of love when bees thrum
and bears rummage through trash cans—
I do not want these barren truths.

Pressing my face to the cool windowpane,
I flash to the second I fell into this fragile world
through the riot of my mother's thighs—
her body ripe with both agony and bliss.
How we come back to this paradox
again and again. How I stand now beneath
the infinite sky, on this pilgrimage
to nowhere beyond *here*. Ask for more.

reflections
~What paradoxes live in your body and in your life?
~When or where in your life have you felt agony and bliss at the same time?

Winter's Dreaming

Here, in the still point between
hibernation and emergence
down deep in the soils
seeds stir and tremble
in the lengthening light.

What it is to trust this gestation—
the fullness of this space
that will birth us again
from mystery into form,
from the wild wordless hum

of no-thing into full symphony.
This morning I awoke to feel
the soft curled petals
of the inner worlds just beginning
to unfurl—ribbons of flame,

a fire burning on low, underground.
I bowed down in thanks
for this delicious slow approach of spring,
for these revelations that come
one tender leaf at a time.

reflections
~How do you value (or resist) times of gestation and stillness, when your life includes less external activity?
~What is opening in you, now—one tender leaf at a time?

Solstice

Days are brief interludes
between the quiet hands of night,
the earth tilting away from the sun.
Fields lay fallow—only the skeletons
of last year's harvest exposed,
the bones of the frosted land.

Pale skies draw us inward
to the place of no speaking, no words—
to stillness where we wait
in the threshold between worlds.
Here there is the deep sea of ourselves,
the strange fish of our dreams.

This is the place of incubation,
where all appears lifeless and barren,
as if it gestates nothing but space.
Rest in the node between in-breath and out-breath.
You need not do anything, but wait
for the pull of your own north star.

See it in the sky now?
It knows your naked beauty,
your clear vessel thirsting for light.
For even now you are pregnant—
full of the just forming, the newly given-
the exquisite bird of your soul.

Soon she will emerge—first beak, then wing,
until she breaks from the center of the egg
and kisses your life, showing you how
to live inside your own luminous skin.

reflections
~What is it like for you to spend more time in the "being" rather than the "doing"?
~When you listen to the silence within, where is your North Star directing you?

Clematis

When I reach into the soil
I reach for stars—the miracle

of seed swelling itself into flesh. When
I search for you in the middle of the night

I move towards the beyond—the curve
of your hip a valley I have walked over

and over like a nomad. The cottonwoods
shed their fluffy seed, the tender grass bolts,

the press of summer is upon us. I shift plants
in moonlight to act out this restless stirring

to spread beyond first planting. Tonight
your fingers rub tomato vines, trace the tendrils

of clematis dancing up the lattice on the axis
of the sky. Already we have forgotten

the barren nights. And in the fullness
of this heat, we stand on teetering apple ladders,

reaching for the fruit just beyond the green fur
of leaf—our want a kite tugging to get off its leash.

Then where would we go? Would we find sky
in that floating? Or would we long only for our feet

on the ground, hands in the earth, mouth
upon mouth in a wild, unweeded garden?

reflections
~What is your relationship to your own longing, eros and sensuality?
~How does your relationship with the natural world feed and nourish your sensual self?

Rewilding

How is it that we become tame?
How is it that we throw off our original skin
for another—leave behind our fur and hooves

and forget the cord of our primary belonging?
As a child you sat often at the roots
of a sycamore tree. In the rustle of those leaves,

you knew that someone had claimed you—
that you could never be cast out of the garden.
But time warps light, sound, memory.

What was once known becomes simply
a flicker of a photograph—a forgotten myth
cast aside for some other truth we think

we must journey far and wide to find.
And that is the way of things, traveler.
Yes, that is the way we wind around

the pathways of our life—up the switchbacks
and down the valleys. *No place to lay my head*,
we cry, as we traverse the high mountain passes.

And this is divine mercy—that all the places
we hope will save us, elude us—until we let them go.
Around the fire one night, under the blaze

of our galaxy's spiral, you saw the untamed one
of you streak across the sky like a comet. In that moment
you knew that you have never been lost,

that you can never be exiled. In that moment
you saw that it is you who longs for *you*—
and that it is your own hands that offer

your thirsty one
a dipper full of stars.

reflections
~In the course of your life, where have you become tame and given up your wildness?
~How can you give yourself the very nourishment you have been looking for in other places or people?

A Way of Walking

There is a way of walking
from one place to another
as if there is nothing
of significance in between.

We have been taught to move
in straight lines, to lay life out
along a grid of efficiencies.
But there is another way to traverse.

This way carves a serpentine road
full of mysterious meetings.
Along this path, the directives come
from the world itself speaking

through all of its voices. And because
you are following some other kind
of guidance—because you are *listening*—
at the next crossroads you turn left

instead of right—and you find yourself
skirting along the edge of a village,
where an old man is harvesting golden apples—
and without a word, he offers you one.

And over the hills, cowbells sound out
like ancient monk song, and the last of the sunlight
breaks through the rainclouds, so that everything
is shimmering—luminous and awake.

And the oak tree that cracked in last night's storm
is dripping with honeycomb and bee hum.
And this moment swells and blooms open
with its own fullness—and you laugh

at the idea of Point A & Point B.
For now you have no idea who you are
or if you have arrived—you only know
that you are everywhere.

reflections
~*How have you laid your life out on a "grid of efficiencies"—what has been the result?*
~*How is the world speaking to you on a daily basis—and what do you hear when you listen?*

creatiOn

House of Origin

Riverswept, we lay down
on the mossy bank,
beaded dragonflies darting gold—
man-boy and woman-girl finding
the song of the body for the first time.

Even now, every time I love
I return to that moment—
that house of origin,
the day we picked blackberries
until our hands were stained.

In the heat of noon
we found a lake, dove in
and entered our own green myth,
the whole of the undressed sky above.
Here, our skin gleamed silver

just beneath the surface. Here,
the perfection of throat and palm
were more than enough. Waterworn
stone, sun on bare tangled limbs—this
is how we drifted through eternity.

Days and nights passed quickly—
until years later, the hoof of the world
came down between us,
and we forgot the shimmering lake
where we came from that day.

Even now, this is the story
that made us—and all others just
possibilities, our lives grown also
from what is unsaid, unwalked.
Even now, this origin story is *true*—

not undone, when the river
of our one life split down
two different canyons.
Even now, this story is a sanctuary—
a place where, for all time,

I kneel before a deep, clear pool,
scooping sweet water to my lips.

reflections
~What are the core personal stories or myths in your life that have made you who you are?

~When have you continued to experience deep love or connection with another person who is no longer in your present day life? How does this impact you?

Arrival

Think of it—the way they made you
        with their bodies. Under this same moon
and stars whirling towards one another

at the speed of love. It takes millennia
        for two galaxies to collide and merge.
Think of the way they poured into each other—

a moment nothing can undo. Then flesh
        out of flesh, mitosis—the embryo translating
codes—fish, amphibian, reptile, mammal—

 the thick fur down your soft spine.
        And as you slowly woke to this life, how you
drank the rose womb light, heard ribbons

of voices outside the whoosh and whomp
        of coursing blood. Yes, this is where you began—
you the laughing shadow on the porch,

where they sat and talked in the cricket
        beating heat, looking out and out—not knowing
you were already here in a cell boat, becoming.

reflections
~What is the story of your own conception?
~What miraculous (and perhaps "ordinary") moments from your own life evoke awe or wonder?

Current

Today, when my son and I return
to the winding river, I remember how,

long ago, we walked here each morning
through speckled forestlight—I, singing to him—

the earth's secrets before us: spotted bodies
of salamanders, the globes of mayapples,

the dense secrets of mud and reeds.
I did not believe we would ever leave

that place, or those primordial days
that merged one into the other—

he edging out further and further
from my body, until he wandered out

of that first fluid dream into the named world.
And it was in those woods one summer—

as he thrust his tiny hand into streamflow,
released his maple leaf boat and watched

it disappear around the bend—that I first saw
an image of him now, a man-boy emerging

before me to say: *here is the green heart of me,
put it in the current so it can swim.*

reflections
~When did your young "green" heart enter life's bigger current, so you could learn to swim?
~When have you let go of a phase of life, an era of a relationship, or a bond with another so that necessary growth could happen

Eleven

It is something about her long limbs, her hair
blowing free in the wind, her unabashed smile.
She, eleven—and still untouched by the shame
that comes later, after our first bloom.

For how many times does a woman
apologize for herself in a lifetime?
How many times do we bow our heads
when we feels eyes upon us, or eclipse our power

so we are not the only starlight in the dark night
of a room? How many ways do we shove
our song in a pocket, lest it attract
too much attention? Or do we simply learn

to pick and probe and alter our beauty
so that it is packaged, easy, comfortable—
so that it does not disturb? But my daughter
knows none of this now—and when I look

into her eyes—I see the Grand Canyon inside her—
ravines full of moonlight, underground caverns
housing thousands of bats that fly out
in the dusk. And the spring in her heart—

sweet water pouring straight from the ground.
Yes, I see a vast mystery I have never seen before.
For I thought I knew all of her—
blood of my blood, but now I see I never will.

For here she is, unfolding delicate wings
she does not even know she has,
preparing to leap into the vast unknown—
to claim all that is hers to claim.

reflections
~What brilliance lives in the hidden depths of you that you tend to hide or eclipse for other people's comfort?
~How do we consciously release and support the children in our life as they leap into the vast unknown?

The Library of the Body

The library of the body is a revelation.

Today I pull out the book of grief
and find one hundred chapters.
There is the chapter on letting go~
where brilliant leaves,
tumble down the branches
of the page, veins lined in gold.

The book of rage comes next.
Rage at the song we could not sing.
Rage at the father who broke our spirit.
Rage at the lover who left us on our knees.
Rage at the god who would not lift us easily
above the rough waters of this world.

This book laughs—throaty and guttural—
and then begins to weep. For such losses
are not simply to be cast off and forgotten.
Here you light a candle as you read
and burn each page as you go on.

Then there is the book of joy.
This book has no words.
This book simply pours
moonlight across your skin.
This book sprouts roses
when you are not looking.

And when you have finished every volume,
the whole of the library unfolds itself
into a trembling forest, and each book
becomes a gleaming apple on the tree of life
that whispers—eat, taste, nourish.

reflections
~*What stories and images live in your book of grief? Your book of rage? Your book of joy?*
~*When you consider the library of your body in its wholeness—what wants to be remembered, seen and honored?*

Net of Dreams

Catkins drape from the willows outside,
    and when I unfold you from sleep,
        pollen dusts the creases of your eyes.

Look, the fleeting earth underfoot,
    the savored moment already gone,
        the lilac blush a stain on the sidewalk.

And this word peony is a round blossom
    dissolving in your mouth, the petals
        tearing away in sudden wind. Days become weeks,

the frothing rush of the snowmelt swollen creek
    slowing to a gentle sway. Yes, this end of us is always
        wanting more, trying to sew eternity godfast

to this body—to hold onto bone mass, muscle tone,
    the steady throb of the electric heart—to make it all stay.
        But already we are pulling away from our old selves—

the years flashing by like street signs. Already, we are not
    what we thought we were—each of us, a shining net of dreams
        casting out into the world—catching for a moment—

    shivering light, dandelion wisps, beads of rain.

reflections
~How have you changed over time? What endures and what cannot last?
~How can the awareness of impermanence support you to savor what is present here and now?

Visitation

When death came to my door
she came softly—her presence startling
me from sleep to the sight of her
standing in the threshold,
a swirling blur of stars
against the pitch of night.

For it was a winter new moon
and her scent like the vanilla
of pinebark on a late summer eve—
her curious gaze penetrating
every hidden place in me.

It was as if she had decided
to stop by to introduce herself—
to come to know me better—
my angel of death. For a moment
I could not breathe—as I knew
I must both honor her
and send her on her way.

And a voice I did not know
rose up in me—booming out
to say: *It is not my time—*
not here, not now—there are seasons
to taste and grandchildren
to cradle and places within
and without to mend.

And when I finished, she nodded
with a sliver of a smile—as if she knew
this was just how this would go.
For somehow in my claiming—
we had made an agreement.

And as her silver silhouette receded—
the dawn's first songbirds called
back the light— and I held
my own precious body and wept.

reflections
~What is your relationship to death and dying?
~How can our angel of death be any ally in our life?

Lineage

In the dream, I was gifted an ornate box,
intricately carved with the songlines
of my ancestors—a box that carried
the scent of sweet wood and the laughter
of all the women who had come before me.

But when I opened the box—
It was an arrow of pain that entered
my body, pierced my heart,
took me to my knees. Feeling
my own life draining away, I called

for my children to say goodbye.
And as I grieved this loss,
welling inside me was a voracious rage,
an impulse to curse those who had cursed me—
for this was not my burden to carry.

But in that moment, my lineage
encircled me and spoke, saying—
this is how it has gone for centuries—
this is how cycles of pain are passed on:
when you give over your power,

when you feed the dis-ease with venom,
when we add poison to poison,
and lash out like a wounded animal on attack.
They showed me how to send the arrow
back to the center of the center of creation

with all the love I had in me.
And with every prayer that came
from my lips, my strength returned—
as I was cleared of the old shadows,
the twisted stories, the phantoms

of helplessness—and was filled instead
with healing waters from the well
where these ancient ones went to drink.
In this way, I was restored again.
And the lineage encircled me saying—

Do you see? The box was the gift that saved your life.
And looking into the eyes of my children
and into the eyes of their children,
I opened my arms to the whole of this truth—
how the curse becomes the blessing,

how the heart transmutes the fiercest
of stings into sweet medicine.

reflections
~*How has your heart transmuted the fiercest stings into sweet medicine?*
~*How does our own personal healing affect our entire lineage—backwards and forwards in time?*

Creation Stories

i.
It wasn't long ago
when humans and bears were one clan,
when in the winter freeze
down in the hibernation caves
dreaming would happen both ways—
from bear to human and human to bear.
In this way, they kept their relations intact
and remembered together what it is
to live in sacred reciprocity with this world.

ii.
I can still feel that first flicker
of my son's body swimming in my own—
a miraculous sea creature in the depths of me.
An exquisite intimacy—
this kind of silent communion.
Daily, we took long walks in the forest,
my hands on my ripe belly,
I whispering secrets to him
that I have never told another.

iii.
In the early dawn light
a baby hummingbird flew into a window,
dropped to the ground in a dark heap.
I picked her up in my hands—and still,
for moments, she did not stir.
It was only when I placed her heart to mine,
blew my breath into her feathers,
that she trembled again with her own life.
How many times have I flown
into that same glass, thinking it was sky?

iv.
When you held me like that
in the middle of the night
in the middle of a dream
when I had forgotten my own name,
it was like touching starlight for the first time.
It's been a long, fierce voyage, I said,
tracing the fine line of your spine,
remembering the boat of my body
sailing in the sea of eternity.
Even with this tattered sail
and bruised hull, I remember how
to ride these storm-tossed waves.

v.
It wasn't long ago
when humans and eagles were one clan
and flew on spirals of currents,
weaving in and out of lifetimes
in the golden light. *This freedom is all there is—*
we cried as we soared—burning feathers
in the sun one last time, before trading
our eternal flight for limbs to walk
the fragrant meadows of this earth,
to know root and bone as home,
and learn the heart's morse code
of longing and wonder.

reflections
~What personal creation myths live at the center of your soul?
~What are you learning about the "heart's morse code of longing and wonder?"

Remembering our Descendants

The day comes when you realize
you are not young anymore, at least
not in the way you thought you would stay.

The wheel turns, the circle widens
and you now occupy a simpler place—
the illusion of your importance dissolving

until you see that you are more a field of light
than the flaming arrow that once burned a hole
through the sky. After the inevitability of our fall,

of our *many* falls, after the surrender
to our own exquisite dismemberments,
we know we are not any of the identities

that have ever claimed us. Ever.
Some things *are* created and destroyed—
and this life is a long kiss that opens us

to the beauty of our own disaster
and inevitability of our exquisite return.
We know the way grief and ecstasy

couple again and again, like two hawks
spiraling up the current. And from those heights
we cry out, as we see our own changing face

in the waves, in the wildflowers, in our children
running full stride in the fields of the earth.
And in this harvest of our life, we feed the world

with our offerings, fully given. And the rest, the chaff,
goes back into the fire that sustains those who will come
long after we are gone from this place.

If only we could wear these wings of our second life
with merciful ferocity—and live as the ancestors
our descendants will remember

as the ones who *would not turn away*
from the impossible, or give up when all seemed lost.
Yes—as the ones who held nothing back,

as they rode through the center of the storm—
forever tending what matters most.

reflections
~What kind of "exquisite dismemberments" have you experienced in your life?
~What do you wish to offer the world from the harvest of your life? What are you fiercely tending?

The Feast

It is green and teeming again,
the soils supple after years of drought—
after the parched places
called like a lover for rain,
after empty reservoirs
filled overnight, and the earth
offered her great generosity
so that everything is opening,
blooming, gleaming
with honeyed light.

There is so much
we could resist in this life—
drought and famine and flood,
the shift of every season,
the arrival of each decade,
the falling away of a lover,
our own aging bodies, every betrayal
or hurt we have ever held close.
We could spend every moment resisting.

For this mammalian heart aches—
we attach, hold on, scan the field
for potential loss. We love so intensely,
we push love away—lest it break us.
And yet to inhabit this body
in every cell, with no holding back,
we cannot avoid touching those
trembling notes of our impermanence—
those strands in our lives
that arrive for a time, but cannot stay.
We cannot avoid risking *everything*.

For in this exquisite love affair
the world will court us again and again—
and in this awakening of spring,
we will forget the other seasons of lack—
as we are reborn, renewed, unwrapped.
And the heat of earth's wild eros
will rise through us—the poppies
bursting their seams, the fillies
cantering in the just born grasses,
the creeks racing high and fast.

And we will think—yes, perhaps it will
always be like this—now that I have
emerged from this *final* winter of my soul.
But all of our seasons will come
around again—grief and passion
and fear, loneliness and ecstasy—
they will all barge in through our back door.
And perhaps, in our forgetting,
we will be surprised by these
familiar strangers who come
in the dark hollow of the night—

or perhaps we will remember this feast
we were invited to long ago—
and we will lay the table
with devotion, pour the wine,
and exhale in awe with all
that is offered—here, now, for all time.

reflections
~*What aspects of life do you still resist—and how does this impact you?*
~*What have you come to understand from moving through season after season of your life?*

Forgiveness

When I first birthed a child,
a ferocious love awoke in me—
so strange and wild
I knew I could kill
for what I loved.
A paradox it seems—
this vow that would have us
tear our own heart out
when a lover dies,
pull a baby from a burning car,
lay our life down for another.

This is the beginning
of understanding sacrifice—
that prayer which says
*take me, only leave
this precious other alone.*
And yet we cannot save
our loved ones from pain.

We wear this body as a cloak
for a time, only to shed it
when the time comes.
And this life of ours is a ship
that drives up against the rocks
until we crack, until we offer
the spring water from our hearts
until we say, *I surrender. I am yours.*

And for all of our lives,
we give and are gifted
in a kind of sacred reciprocity—
until the lines in our face
become the scripture of a life
that has come full circle—
until tears well simply
from the poignancy of things,
and from this knowing in the bones
that nothing can be lost
and that all is forgiven.

reflections
~What does the idea of sacrifice mean to you? Where have you sacrificed for another?
~What losses are you still grieving or holding on to? Where is forgiveness called for?

a w a k e n in g

The Boat

You have not missed the boat.
You are not late to the party.
You have not taken the wrong turn,
or the wrong ticket, or ended up
in the wrong line. You have not made
the fatal mistake that will destroy you
for all time. You haven't undershot
the bullseye or slept through the final
moments of the ultimate opportunity.
You have not missed the boat.

You are the boat—
and the sea that gently tugs
on the moorings, unties the knots—
and in its time, when the wind is right—
releases you to the drawing tide.
For you know this open water
and this joy that breaks free for no reason—
you know this unmovable peace
that arises in spite of storms
and high seas and even the terrible
losses that seem unbearable.

For there is all that comes and goes,
and there is that which is indestructible—
the essence that changes forms
but does not die. There is the one of you
who laughs at the impossibility
of being human—to be wired like this:
with the hurricane of the mind
and the tiger of the heart,
and the rise and fall of the passions
moving in us like sweet fire.

Yes, you are not the one running
for the boat that is leaving the port—
not the one who is seconds too late
for your life. Nor the one debating
which way to go, or frantically seeking
the ultimate truth. You are not even
the one trying so hard to find
the last piece of the puzzle
that would make you whole.

You *are* the boat
and this drawing tide.

reflections
~When in your life have you felt like you "missed the boat?"
~What supports you to relax your seeking, so you can receive the whole of your life with open arms?

Surrender

There are moments when—
no matter how deeply you love
the holy wholeness of your life—
something quakes along the fault lines,
some grace that feels like a curse
taps along the fissures,
some alchemy of soul fire and magma
builds beneath the tectonic plates
of all you have created—
and in a moment *everything* shifts.

And your heart, which is broken,
realizes that the prayer it has sung
is returning as a kind of unexpected
answer to a question,
a light to a dark mystery
you have been seeking to understand—
only this was never the way
you imagined the song ending.
And you have spent days
and weeks and months watching

the fissures widening, crying out
to have the strength to mend and fuse.
But now the chasm has opened
beyond any hope of repair,
and the singing waters of destiny
rise up through the cracks—
and this river of elation
surges through you.
And you weep and tremble
at the same time—

for this is the fierce revelation
of your unexpected life—
and there is nothing
to do but surrender.

reflections

~When have you tried to hold onto something in your life that simply needed to fall apart?

~What gifts have these moments of dissolution or falling apart brought to you? What part of your "unexpected life" do you now have access to that you wouldn't otherwise?

Heart Sutra

Beyond hope and fear
good and bad
low road or high road
curse or blessing
there is this moment—
this invitation to arrive
on your knees,
in your glory
awake.

The forestlight trembles
the mountains surge and quake
the meadows exhale wildflowers—
for even as you see, you are seen.
As you bless, you are blessed.
As you drink, you are drunk.
Nothing is outside of this.

Even when
we are dismantled
bone by bone
cell by cell
and taken back
into creation's great belly
there is no where to go.

I once dreamed
we were a winged people
who had forgotten our wings
and then designed a whole world
whose sole purpose
was our re-membering.

Can you see us—
violet feathers
silver sky
singing on the wind?

reflections
~What exists beyond hope and fear, good and bad, curse or blessing?
~What have you come to re-member in this lifetime?

Alchemy

We wake from the dream
and cannot remember.
How many times in a lifetime
does this happen—
where we rise with the taste
of the other world sweet
on the tongue and no memory
of where we have been?

But within this temple of here
there is the low cooing of doves
in the morning, the sun on bare limbs
as we stir. All along the path of now
there is bread on the water,
water into wine, the miracle
of crimson buds on the branches,
the springflow we thirst for swelling
through every crack and crevasse.

But even with all of this,
there are moments when we long
to escape the ache of embodiment,
to return to the communion
we remember in dreams, in flashes
of our star-sung origins.

This is the tender alchemy
of being human—
what we search for discovered
in the most common blooming—
in these bodies where mortal
and infinite collide.

It is this crucible that first drew us
down the ladder between the worlds
to be pierced by this wild love—
to feel more than we thought
we could bear, to know ourselves
as empty and full all at once,
with nothing to hold onto.

reflections
~How do you experience the "tender alchemy of being human"—of being both mortal and infinite?
~How have you been pierced by the Wild Love of this world—and how has that changed you?

Love Poem from God

The heart is a sitar longing
for the last note of resolution
that never comes—

and the soul is a thunder clap
of stillness that awakens
the drunk and the numb.

The sun will rise and set on us.
Here, everything is given,
and nothing withheld.

And you, you are all
you think you cannot bear—
you are the wandering saint

and the broken denier.
You are the gravity of love
that sears and repairs all at once.

And it is in the tasting of the wine
of your own darkness and light
that you are set free!

reflections
~How are you "all that you think you cannot bear"?
~How can the intentional act of tasting the "wine of your own darkness and light" set you free?

Where the Honey is Stored
after Kabir

Beloved, we do not have to do anything to deserve you.
And yet we are always trying to prove ourselves—

looking for meaning, asking about purpose,
when all along we are swimming in the coral reefs

of your warm oceans and tilling the soil for the next
season of waving green rye. This is the home

we have always dreamed of, the garden where we once
saw a no trespassing sign and believed it! The drill

of the mind bores down layers and layers in search
of answers. Meanwhile, an ecstatic dance is unfurling

just outside our thoughts. Nothing to do but love them—
these bees of the mind that buzz in summer flowers.

Quick! Run past the construction sites of the self
to the hive where all the honey is stored!

reflections
~*How have you tried to prove yourself or your own worthiness?*
~*Where are the construction sites of your own self—and where is the honey?*

Without Exile

In the kingdom without exile
there are no borders to defend—
and the soldiers all sling mud
at one another from hilltops,
the way they longed to as boys.

In the kingdom without exile,
even thieves wander the streets
calling for their mothers.
And the addicts, they only want
the taste of god in their mouths—
to drink the green light of forests.

In the kingdom without exile
the daggers of the mind plunge
straight through the soul,
leaving no mark.
The pain pours through.
The fear pours through.
The laughter pours through.
Nothing sticks.

And the dream demons
who shook their death rattles at you
simply crumple into heaps
and turn into butterflies.

And the ones we once wished
to send away live in the center of town—
the drunk, the crazy, the wounded, the sick.
And what would be a hell
becomes a heaven simply
because every one is *seen*.

Come home to this country
without exile. See yourself
mirrored back a thousand times—
you—this surging singing crowd
tearing down the barbed wire.

reflections
~What parts of yourself have you exiled over time? Who in your life have you exiled...and why?
~Who is the "surging singing crowd tearing down the barbed wire"—what have they come to teach you?

Eye of the Moon

1
Sometimes, when all the longing
is wrung out of my soul
I lie down in the tall grasses
beneath Venus and the crescent moon
and breathe in the quiet. And I see
that all that is within me
that wants to run fast and far
is on a road to nowhere—
and this tender flickering of silver light
against blue-black night
is enough to live on for a lifetime.

2
Sometimes when we have climbed
far and wide above the valley of our life
and gotten drunk on the gin of this thin air,
we gaze down longingly at the fine houses
billowing firesmoke, the flocks of memories
nested in the limbs of trees,
the lean muscled bravado
of our own youth, and we wonder
how it is that we can ever walk out
of any of life's doors without running
back to the gods of time, begging:
please, let me stay just a little bit longer.

3
Sometimes, when god's ferrymen
have rowed the spirit boats
long and hard into the sea of stars,
there is a moment when, *all together now,*
they pause, oars lifted—a caesura
of breath and water droplets glistening.
And a sigh breaks over the bow
as the reflection of our one original face appears
clear and true in these ancient waters—
and even the most hardened warriors weep.

4
Sometimes, when we finally meet
the ones we knew we would someday find,
we look up into the eye of the moon
and say, thank you for sending down
these silver ladders of remembrance.
And then we take turns climbing,
rung over rung, your hands and then mine,
up and down the passageways
between the worlds.

5
Sometimes, when the last card
has been played, when we are empty handed,
sure we will never escape alive—
an angel of mercy appears on the horizon
riding bareback in the dawn,
and we know the darkest hour
has passed. And just as we cry out,
convinced we have been forgotten—
we are found. And just as we
stop fighting against our bindings,
we realize we have always been free.

reflections
~What are the moments in your life that you never want to leave behind and wish
 you could experience again?
~When are the times in your life when you were convinced you were lost—
 and then later discovered you were found?

Luminous

There is a place within
that cannot be destroyed
by flood or fire,
by bloodthirsty armies
or devastating illness—
it this untouchable essence
that quakes with irrepressible light
and bears the intolerable weight
of all we must feel to awaken.

When I first found myself again
after surgery, my own name strange,
both of my breasts removed—
I did not feel loss or grief,
but a love so ferocious, it rolled
through me like thunder,
bringing healing rain.

After that, came a knowing
of my own wholeness
beyond any story—this revelation
of the luminous body—
innocent and unharmed in spite
of all of our sacred shatterings.

And yes, now the landscape
is unrecognizable—yes, now,
there is no old path to go back to—
yes now, the quivering arrow
of this moment pierces the heart—
the illusion of invulnerability
stripped away. And so it is.

Before I came to this life,
I was shown this world
from the distant shores of it—
and in that moment I saw
the full arc of my days here,
the exquisite range
of this embodied dreaming.
Oh how beautiful, I cried.
Oh how terrible.
Oh—this terrible beauty.

And the angel who guided me
simply pointed to the shimmering
horizon and said—*Yes.*

reflections
~What is the place within you that cannot be destroyed?
~How has life brought you "terrible beauty?"

The Empty Bowl

For Teresa

A woman of courage tells me:
*After illness, I placed
an empty glass bowl
in the center of my room,
in the center of my life—
and each day I watched
my own desire to fill it again.*

I know this empty bowl she speaks of—
for it is turning in the center
of my heart. And the fire that burns
in that space is so hot, I want to do
anything to stop the searing—
to fill the bowl again by adding,
bit by bit—all the old pieces of myself,
all the familiar roles and tasks—
to reassemble the known elements
and recreate what the fire
has forever undone.

But today, in this early dawn –
the bowl shimmers with first light.
It has become a kind of prism
reflecting what is true beyond names.
and though at times the space
feels like an ache or a void,
I begin to know it as an offering
from the source of Life itself—
an offering I have refused
so many times before.

And so this morning
I am ready to receive
what has been given—
to lift the bowl to my lips
and taste the nectar
of a new kind of belonging
that is no longer about
perfecting the storyline
or proving the myth of invulnerability.

Yes, I have placed an empty bowl
in the center of my life,
in the center of my heart—
and I will not fill it with the debris
of the past—but will cherish
this clear vessel brimming
with infinite sky, and the voice
inside that whispers—
from here, everything is possible.

reflections
~What roles do you need or wish to let go of in your life right now?
~When you let go of who you have been & what you thought you needed to be, what is possible in your life?

The Ocean Inside
after Hafiz

"The Beloved has gone completely Wild – He has poured Himself into me! I am Blissful and Drunk and Overflowing." **From *The Great Secret* by Hafiz**

The Beloved says: *there is an ocean inside you—*
and all it takes to swim here is to surrender.
And you who have become a master
of delving the depths, shedding skin
after skin, letting go of the old,
rising up from your own phoenix ash—
you say, *oh yes, I know this infinite sea.*

But the Beloved says—wait, there is more.
For still, within you there have been hold outs—
places that brace against the harsh boot
of the world. Tensile webs protecting
intricate chambers from desecration.
Secret caves where hidden jewels shine.
And no, it will not be the crack of the hammer,

or the cruel weight of a cruel god,
or the sweltering heat that binds you
into submitting to this ocean. Nor will it be
the *will* of any other who convinces—
but simply the lion's roar of an unfettered
love so freely given, you simply
remember the ocean that you are.

This is how the heat of the divine within
grows from a flicker to a hot holy fire—
this is how stars bloom from the void
and forests grow from broken open husks.
This is the way the Beloved woos you
into tasting your own nectar,
into entering the very blossom

of the milky way. Yes, this is the way
the beloved points you home.

reflections
~Where are the "hold outs" within you—places that you have kept secret, hidden, protected?
~Currently, how is the Beloved—the divine within—pointing you home?

Cornucopia

Out of the empty vessel, the riot of the earth's wild feast
laid before us daily, in places we have forgotten
to look. In the veins of the leaf in the sunlit corner

of the room. In the depths of the tiger iris of the daughter
who has grown into a woman overnight. In the clear pools of water
where night animals bend down and drink.

If we have any task it is this: to live in this exquisite seeing,
to clear our eyes of the dust of memory and expectation
that would leave us blind to what we most long for.

Even in the leanest of years, when our bodies are wracked
with grief, there is more than enough beauty to feed
all the species of this world. Take the Pleides.

Take Jupiter arcing west in the night sky. Take, the bees
 that roll over on the flowers drunken with nectar. Take the globes
of squash and the sage brush in the russet hills. Take it all in.

For even in the bones and cinders of the old world children reach
into pockets for marbles and a man gives another man his coat.
Even in the skeletal remains of fields gone fallow, seeds settle

and germinate. This cornucopia is what you have come for—
this chance to tend the life within and without, to give back
to that which gives, to be breathed one breath at a time.

reflections

~How can you cultivate a state of "exquisite seeing"—where your vision is clear of "the dust of memory and expectation that would leave us blind to what we most long for?"

~How are you called to "tend life within and without—to give back to that which gives?"

About **Luminous**

The Title

For me, luminosity is the quality of intrinsic radiance that lives in all sentient beings. The title of this collection is meant to acknowledge the wholeness of our being that is woven from both our "light" and our "dark." In our world, dominant culture privileges the light—and fears and avoids the dark—within and without. By darkness, I am both speaking about the night time or the black of an unlit room—as well as to the dark fertile earth, the dark matter of the universe, the dark and unknown spaces within, and the void—the space of pure potential and birthplace of all of creation. For me, the dark also refers to our individual and collective "shadow"—the unclaimed, unremembered or invisible aspects of ourselves that we hide, sequester or suppress because of shame, vulnerability, or fear of exile. Shadow often includes our intuition, wildness, sensuality, sexuality, and unique ways of knowing (beyond our rational and linear understandings). In my experience, our luminosity flowers from our understanding and embrace of both the light and the dark—in ourselves and the world. This collection of poems explores the "soul alchemy" that emerges from this life-long journey.

The Luminous Body

At 47, I was diagnosed with Stage Two breast cancer. When I underwent surgery just six weeks after diagnosis—I was given a profound gift upon waking. As my consciousness returned, I had an overwhelming and visceral understanding of my luminous body—the aspect of us that is always whole and radiant, no matter what has "happened" to us. I woke up from surgery in ecstasy—knowing nothing had been lost and that all was profoundly well. I felt how my luminous body was completely held and supported in a web of Love. In fact, I experienced my luminous body (and all of our luminous bodies) as Love itself.

Two years after my initial diagnosis, just before the publication of this book, I experienced a recurrence of breast cancer. I now daily call upon this image of my luminous body and connect to the infinite field of Love where everything is possible.

Loving Acknowledgements

Thank you to the Muse, who first made herself known when I was just a young sprite dancing around the kitchen, pondering the source and meaning of Life. At six, those musings became my first poems.

Thank you to my wise and wonderful adult children who have brought me such joy and inspiration. I love you with all my heart.

Thank you to my marvelous blended family, who has supported me and enriched my life always.

I am eternally grateful to my mother Pam Hale Trachta—who has read every poem I ever wrote and watered the seeds of my expression with love all along the way.

I give thanks to my exquisite circle of brilliant and radiant women. Every woman needs doulas, co-conspirators, and truth-tellers in her life to birth her creations into the world.

Thanks to the *Lifting the Veils*™ women—who first engaged with these poems in our retreats together—you are remarkably brave and beautiful beings.

A special shout out to Tryshe Dhevny **(SoundShifting.com)** for her collaboration on our *Lifting the Veils* CD—that includes Tryshe's exquisite vocals and crystal bowls, alongside my readings of seven poems from **Luminous**. This collaboration also includes marvelous meditations by my mother Pam Hale. The links to tracks from *Lifting the Veils* are on my website **LuminousPoetry.com**.

Thank you to all who have read, listened to and reflected on these poems—and encouraged me to create a book that could be a physical, living, breathing, singing offering. You are the wind in my wings and the creative spirits who inspire me.

Thank you to my champion and book angel—designer Suzanne Nason with Twistology—your passion, creative vision, skillfulness and steadfast belief in this project has been beyond inspiring. Without you, this beautiful book would not have found its truly exquisite form.

Thank you to our ancestors who have gifted us with blessed wisdom traditions and essential roadmaps for this Mysterious life—and to the bards and poets and mystics and wild ones who have kept soul language alive through so many eras and eons.

Thank you to my descendants—who have continually whispered in my ear, saying—don't ever give up on dreaming the new dream of this world.

Thank you to the powerful, beautiful and challenging experiences and initiations that have shaped me—without you, I would not know my own unique song—with all of her chords of joy, grief, tenderness, and ecstasy.

Thank you to the Divine Mystery for the Eternal Dance.

Praise for **Luminous**

"**Luminous** is a precious gem, a masterpiece of loveliness, a deep dive into the soul. The poems in this book will enlighten, nourish, support and envelope you. Laura has written a gift relevant to all people—but particularly to seekers, awakened ones and people committed to their constant growth and development. It is a treasure."
~Lynne Twist, Author of *Soul of Money* & Co-Founder, Pachamama Alliance

"Laura's poems are magical adventures. Like shamanic journeys, they inspire us to soar through portals to our higher consciousness. We reawaken to our connection with nature, the earth and the universe."
~John Perkins, Author of *Confessions of an Economic Hitman, The Secret History of the American Empire, The World as You Dream It* and many more

"**Luminous** is a collection of poems that have arrived out of Laura's deep kinship with nature—both the outer landscape and the inner seasons of the soul's unfolding. With an attentiveness to their contours, rhythm and flavour, it's as if the poet reunites words until their combined picture emerges—and we unexpectedly, gratefully find ourselves in it."
~Toko-pa Turner, Author of *Belonging: Remembering Ourselves Home*

"Laura Weaver is fluent in the language of the heart—the heart that knows the beauty and joy of being touched by the seasons of time, the pain of loss, the rootedness of the natural world, and the delicacy of stillness. I suspect that like me, her poetry will authentically touch your heart in a way that you too feel seen and known."
~Michael Stone, Journalist and Host and Producer of *The Shift Network Shamanism Global Summit* and *KVMR's Conversations*

"A poet of the soul, Laura Weaver's **Luminous** is an invitation to hold sacred the truth of our vulnerabilities—our greatest strength. Every word is a carrier wave delivering intricate sound codes that awaken the mystery and mastery of a human life."

~Tryshe Dhevney, *Sounds True* Recording Artist, Sound Healer, Actor & Director

"There is nowhere to hide in Laura Weaver's exquisite poetry. **Luminous** shines the light on our deepest longings, wounds, joys and sorrows, with no apology. This utterly beautiful collection will break you open—over and over again."

~Pasha Hogan, Author of *The Joy of Creative Discovery* and *Third Time Lucky: A Creative Recovery* and Founder of Creative Discovery

"Laura Weaver's poems are a salve for the human soul. These pages will accompany your path, as they have mine, providing expression for the ineffable, solace for the unbearable, and profound hope and inspiration for what's possible."

~David Tucker, Pachamama Alliance

"This is a book of poems that I want to show my mother, my daughter, my grandmother—and bask in their aching, loving truths and insights."

~Rebecca Ghanadan, PhD, Founder, Aspis Coaching Group

"Laura Weaver's book of poetry, **Luminous** is a light-filled journey into the deepest recesses of our heart and soul. The words and images remind us to be hopeful in the vast mystery of life. This collection could easily be used as part of a daily meditation ritual."

~Diane S. Turner, LCSW, CLC, Author, *Heart Wisdom, A Concise Companion for Creating a Life of Possibility*

LAURA **WEAVER**

Laura Weaver, MA, is a poet, author, teacher, guide, and organizational consultant with over two decades of experience in writing, education, leadership, healing, and non-profit and social change work. Over the last twenty-five years, Laura has offered courses, retreats, and workshops on women's leadership, poetry and writing, rites of passage, equity, and heart-centered education. She is the co-author of **The Five Dimensions of Engaged Teaching** (*Solution Tree Press 2013*) and has published dozens of poems, book chapters, blogs, and essays. Her experience with her own healing journeys deeply inform her writing and work as a "soul guide" for others who are going through significant passages. Laura has been rooted in Boulder, Colorado for the last twenty years—where she is daily inspired by wide open spaces, audacious wildflowers, coursing snow-fed streams and diamond nights.

For more information on her life and work:

Visit her website at LauraWeaver.org
Visit her book site at LuminousPoetry.com

www.ingramcontent.com/pod-product-compliance
Lightning Source LLC
Chambersburg PA
CBHW031428290426
44110CB00011B/570